Sport is Fun

Dianne Irving

Contents

Sport

We like to play sport.

3

Soccer

Soccer is fun.
I like to play soccer.

I kick the ball.
I hit the net!

Swimming

Swimming is fun.
I like to swim.

I get into the pool.
I kick my legs.

Running

Running is fun.
I like to run.

I run in the park.
I run fast!

Cricket

Cricket is fun.
I like to play cricket.

I get my bat.
I hit the ball hard!

Picture Index